OPTIONS TRADING STRATEGIES 2 EDITION

GW01072145

1

Contents

Introduction

Options trading refer to a contractual agreement between two parties in which the buying party gets the right to trade a security at a predetermined price and at a predetermined date. The right, however, is not obligatory in nature. The right is given to the buyer by the seller through the payment of premiums. Options trading involve trading with stocks and securities for the purpose of profit and also keen to avoid incurring losses. In options trading, the buyer is also referred to as the taker in the contract. The seller is usually referred to as the writer.

Types of Options Trading

There are two types of options trading that grant two different rights. The first one is termed as call options. They give the buyer rights to purchase the asset that is underlying the contract on a later date depending at a predetermined price. This right is, however, not obligatory and is usually based on the discretion of the taker or the contract and his understanding of the market performance in the course of the life of the contract. The life of the contract refers to the period before the contract expires. The price of buying the contract is termed as the exercise price. Sometimes it is also referred to as the strike price.

An example of call options is if Santos Limited has a contract available with shares on security that has the last sale price of $6.00. If the contract has a three-month expiry period, the taker then has the option of offering the shares for a call of $6.00. One can buy 100 token offerings of securities at the said call price per share at the time of choice for the taker in the course of the life of the contract. The taker is also required to pay premiums to the writer of the contract for the option. To fully own the call rights, one has to exercise it based on the predetermined dates that are specified in the agreement.

On the hand, the writer of the contract has an obligation to ensure that the shares that are purchased are delivered. In the above example, the writer has to deliver 100 security token offerings as long as the taker of the contract has exercised the option. However, the writer sustains reception of option premium during the life of the contract regardless of Put whether or not the taker exercises the option.

The other form of options is the put options. These ones are designed to grant the taker rights of selling the underlying assets for a price that has been predetermined by the contract. The rights to sell have to be exercised in the course of the life of the contract. Just like the call options, the taker of the contract is not compelled to exercise the right. In this case, the buyer only provides the shares required in the agreement if the put right is exercised.

An example of a put option is when a contract by the writer has a predetermined $6.00 put token offering for a predetermined period of three months. The taker has a put option of selling 100 security token offerings as shares at the said price of $6.00 per share. This sell right has to be exercised in eth active life of the contract by the date of expiry of the agreement.

As with the call option, the taker still has to pay premiums to the writer for the contract and the trade to be valid. The right is only valid when it is exercised with the course of the life of the contract. Outside of it, the right is forfeited regardless of whether or not value was created out of the contract. This means that the taker of the contract has to be keen on market performance and judge well whether or not to invoke the sell rights and when. Sometimes, a taker will opt not to exercise the right of sale of shares as the contract expiry dies out.

The exercise style is usually dependent on the system used. Two systems are usually used: the American style and the European style. The European style usually compels the taker to exercise the right in the contract only on the expiry date. The American style is more flexible and allows the exercise of the right any time before the date of expiry of the agreement.

Advantages of Option Trading

Option trading has many advantages for investors. Essentially, it is an investment that offers an opportunity for those who have the capital to delve into an income generation venture. Advantages with options trading are multiple and should motivate people into the sector of trading securities, selling and buying assets as well as earning interests that accrue.

First is the ability of this venture to aid to manage risks when investing in stocks and securities. They can cushion one from having to incur losses in investment. This is because investing in the stocks and shares usually involves risks of all in the value of the shares. This devaluation can lead to a dwindling of the profits and may, in fact, cut into the shares that one holds. However, the options marketing ensure that one is hedged from such uncertainty and as well as guarantees that a person can earn value from the trading of the shares.

Options trading is also advantageous is it allows someone the time to decide about purchase or not. This is particularly the advantage of the call options. The contract usually has a period during which a person considers the exercise of the implied rights. The person studies the market and its performance and has the allowance to understand his financial situation before making a decision on whether to purchase the shares or not. This leads one to make decisions about investments that are reasoned out. It always comes with more preparedness to handle the consequences of the decisions that one takes. This helps to rid the habit of making trading decisions on whims that can later lead to anxiety and worry as market forces swing into play.

The freedom of action to exercise an option is also an exciting aspect of trading. This is because this is a speculative filed based on eth analysis of market forces and performance. Once one enters an option contract, they can happily enjoy trading them without the obligation to exercise the rights included in the contract. One can, in fact, just understand the market landscape and opt for a trade investment with an option that one does not even have intentions of exercising. On the speculative conception of options trading, one can decide just to exercise the purchase right in a call option when they know the market environment is getting better and promises value. They can also decide to exercise the sell option when losses are expected to avoid the loss or salvage a profit margin.

Leverage

Leverage is a very beneficial aspect of options trading that people try to take advantage of and participate in the security market. In leverage, one has to place smaller outlays with a prospect of making higher profits in view. This encourages those who do not have the capital to invest in the underlying assets or shares to find a way of investing and get returns. One of the crucial parts of leverage is that one is usually getting back returns from the underlying assets or shares, yet they have not been required to pay the full cost for the purchase of the shares.

In the idea of leverage also is also the advantage of diversification. This by creating a portfolio without incurring huge initial outlays. This diversification can then create a stream of investment channels that in practice, lead to profits increasing one's earnings. Sometimes this income can increase to go above one's dividends when one takes call options that are laid again the shares owned. This extra income can even emanate from the shares that are integrated having been acquired from a lending facility. Option premiums also come ahead of the trading activities and hence cushioning one from any chances of loss.

Components of an Option Contract

There are various standardized components of option contracting that enable ease in engaging in options trading. These components characterize the mechanics of how options trading bind the parties involved and demonstrate the ay profits can be generated if the market forces are favorable. Among the components of options trading is:

- Underlying securities

- Contract size

- Expiry day

- Exercise prices

Underlying securities

Options that are traded on the market only apply to certain assets. These assets are then referred to as underlying securities. The word shares can be replaced with the word shares in certain instances. There are companies that provide the asset against which the option operators list options. ASX is one operator in the options trading market has played a crucial role in the listing of underlying securities.

The term classes of options refer to the listing of puts and calls as options of the same assets. As an example, is when puts and calls are applied to a lease corporation's shares. This does not put in regard the contract terms in terms of the predetermined price or duration of expiry of the call and put contracts. An operator of options trading usually provides the list of the available classes for the benefit of investors.

Contract Size

On the ASX platform of options trading, the market standardizes the size of the option contract at 100 underlying securities. One option contract, therefore, corresponds to 100 underlying shares. The changes that can happen only come when reorganization happens on the initial outlay of the underlying share or the capital therein. Index options usually fix the value of the contract at an individual stipulated dollar rate.

Expiry day

Options are constrained by time and have a life span. There are predetermined expiry deadlines that the platform operator sets which have to be respected. These deadlines are usually rigid, and once they are out the rights under a contract in a particular class of unexercised options are then forfeited. Usually, the last day of the life span of a contract is the summative trading date. For shares that have their expiry coming by June of 2020, the options over them have their last trading day on a Thursday that comes before the last Friday that happens to be in the month. Those that expire beyond June 2020, expiry is on the third Thursday that happens to be in the month. For index options. Expiries come on the concurrent third Thursday of the same month of writing the option. However, these dates can be readjusted by the options platform operator as and when there is a reason for such action.

In recent years, platform operators have introduced more short-term options for some underlying. Some are weekly, while others are on a fortnightly basis. These ones have the corresponding weekly or fortnightly expiries. When the life span of options run out, the operators then creates new deadlines. However, all classes of options have their expiries subject to quarters of the financial calendar.

Exercise Prices

These are the buying price or the price of selling the assets or underlying securities. These prices are also called strike prices. They are usually predetermined in the option contract and have to be met if one has to exercise the rights in an option. Mostly, they are called exercise because the parties are now invoking the rights that are stipulated in an option either to buy or sell. The exercise of the option is, therefore, subject to the price stipulations.

Chapter 1. The Purchase of Options

Why Trade with Options?

Though we understand that "options" give the investor the advantage of getting involved with trading without actually having to buy stocks, there are a few more compelling points as to why one should consider trading with "options".

The scope to speculate is the biggest strength of trading with "options". As was cited in the example above, it is possible for you to speculate as to what the stocks can be worth. If you use your wits and are capable of speculating correctly, you will have a chance to hit the jackpot, all within the same day. A combination of how the price changes within a specific time period plus the commissions involved, plays a high factor in making effective use of speculation for making good money with "options" trading. You will always enjoy speculating and the more you do it, the more you start to predict correctly. Now, don't compare this with "normal" gambling as there, you will have only a few choices to pick from, like picking between teams A and B. Here, the "options" market puts forth an ample number of choices for you to pick from and depending on your choice and needs, you can pick the best stocks and trade with them.

2.   The second good reason is called "hedging". Hedging is nothing but insurance, which is what "options" are to your stocks as they insure you against potential losses that might incur if a stock fails. Though purists in the stock market trading scene may argue that it is unwise to make an investment on

stocks that you think will not reap you profits, there could always be cases where you want to take a risk – for example, with new technology stocks- which could reap huge profits. Attention though is needed, as you cannot always be too sure about them. So instead of not investing at all, "options" are a great way to take careful risks and cushion against any potential failure by using effective hedging strategies. As we saw in the example, a person can make a profit of $1,000 on the investment but will get to save $4,000 on it. So it is a wider choice for you to adopt such a strategy as opposed to "gambling" away your $5,000.

3.   A third reason is that, trading in options presents the opportunity for you to take advantage of the market's unlimited profit potential while enjoying limited risks.

4.   You already know that the buyer of an "options" contract puts down a payment known as premium to the "options" writer or the seller. The amount that the buyer pays is the amount paid for the "option" although there is more about the price. When you pay the premium to an "option" seller, you are not buying anything and no asset will be transferred to you until you decide to exercise the purchase. This is an agreement that lets the buyer choose if and when the transfer of the "option" will take place. However, the underlying asset – the stock, determines the value of the "options" contract. The amount of shares the buyer gets is the number of "option" contracts multiplied by the contract multiplier (also called the contract size). Because small investors can get to take advantage of leveraging – trading extensive

exposure while outlaying only a small amount of capital, this form of investment is beautiful.

Apart from these apparent reasons for trading "options", another attractive characteristic is that a lot of the stock "options" of huge corporations is not available to the public, as they are offered exclusively to the companies' employees via a program called ESP – Employee Stock Program as part of their benefits package. This aspect of exclusivity is a great deal for both; for the companies, in that they get to retain the best talent but also for the employees, who are at an advantage when the company's stocks are doing great.

The employees will work hard towards helping the company making it big. An employee can hold on to the stocks even if he or she quits. Several employees who had invested in companies such as Apple and Microsoft had the chance to sell their stocks once the companies made it big and they became millionaires overnight. Similarly, if your company is offering a chance to buy stocks then you must make use of the opportunity. However, it is important to check whether the stock is doing well in the market. If it is, then you can buy and hold it for a long time. Once the price of the stock reaches its lifetime high, you can decide to sell it in the market and profit from it.

These are just some of the advantages of "options" but it is not limited to these.

This must explain how, when and why to buy options. It must explain what the main reasons why trading options offer a limited investment opportunity, how you can hedge your risks with index funds, how to profit from other losses, collect premiums, capitalize on oversized gains.

We are going to learn what factors influence options pricing and how they do so. It turns out that options pricing is constrained and described by compact formulas, which makes it easy to simulate options behavior using mathematical models and even just Excel spreadsheets. You can find options calculators online that will let you enter in various properties of an option and get estimates as to how its price will change. The two biggest factors that make options prices move include the price of the stock and the passage of time if you understand that then you've grasped 2/3 of what you need to understand to trade options successfully.

Now let us investigate the details when it comes to determining options pricing.

Time Value

Every options contract has time value, but it is also subject to time decay. Time value is the price of the option that comes from the amount of time remaining until the option expires. The time or extrinsic value is not exact and can change based on the price of the option relative to the market. To give an example, the more an option goes into the money, the less it is impacted by time decay. But one thing is certain; all options are impacted by time decay. Simply put, this means that the price of the options will decline as time passes.

For sellers of options contracts, time decay is their best friend. That makes it more likely the options will expire worthlessly, and the option will not be exercised.

For buyers of options contracts, time is your enemy. You are looking to profit before time runs out. Whether or not you can do so will depend on whether the option is in the money or not.

Also, remember that time value is also called extrinsic value. The option also has intrinsic value. This is pricing derived from the underlying stock. Properties that can influence it include price and its properties like the volatility. Extrinsic value comes from the outside.

Let us look at a few examples. In order to understand how things, work, it is helpful to hold variables constant and isolate the variable you are trying to learn about. That is a fictitious example, but once you understand how things work by examining them in isolation, you are going to be far more capable of understanding how the pricing of real options is changing and why.

In this example, we will begin with a stock with a $100 share price with 30 days left before expiration. We will set the implied volatility to 15%.

Let us consider an option which is at the money. If the strike price was $100, the call and the put for this option are priced at $1.78 and $1.76 respectively (remember to multiply by 100 in order to get the actual price you would have to pay to buy the option or the price you'd actually get selling the option).

Now let us see how time decay impacts the option prices. Simply moving to 20 days left to expiration, we find that the price of the call and put options have declined to $1.45 and $1.44, respectively. Both have declined because the strike is equal to the market price, and the only thing impacting the price of the option is time decay. With only 20 days left to expiration, the options have less time value. At this point, 100% of the option value is extrinsic, that is determined by time value.

Now let us shift the clock again, to 10 days to expiration. Now the call option has dropped to $1.03, and the put option is $1.02. At 7 days to expiration, the call option is $0.86, and the put option is $0.85. Moving to 3 days to expiration, the call option and put option are both priced at $0.56. Finally, one day to expiration, the call and put option are both worth $0.32.

Time decay works in exponential fashion. What that means in practice is that the closer that you get to the expiration date, the faster the extrinsic or time value of the option decays.

But let us consider what would happen if the option went in the money, right at the last moment. First, consider what would happen if the stock price went up to $102 a share. In that case, it means the call option is "in the money." We find that the price of the call jumps to $2.00. The put would be virtually worthless.

On the other hand, had the price of the stock dropped by $2; instead, it would be the put that would be priced at $2.00, and the call would be virtually worthless.

Time decay always impacts options, except toward the end the intrinsic value (see below) can overwhelm it. The degree to which it does depends on how far in the money the option price has moved.

Now let us consider an in the money option. First, we will consider a put option, and we will say the stock price is $98 a share, with a strike price of $100. With 30 days left to expiration, the put option is $2.91. The call option is $0.94. So the call option, which is out of the money, is a comparative bargain, and if you are expecting the stock to rise over the succeeding30 days, it could be a good move to buy that call option.

At 20 days to expiration, if nothing else changes (stock price of $98, strike price of $100), the call option is priced at $0.65, and the put option is $2.64. This is an important thing to note – so even though the put option is in the money, we see a price decline. This happens as a result of lost time value.

At 10 days to expiration, the prices of the call and put have dropped to $0.31 and $2.30, respectively. At seven days, the put option is $2.19, and the call option is $0.20. Finally, with two days left to expiration, the put option is $2.02, while the call option is a mere $0.02.

The same thing happens to a call option that is in the money if everything, but time decay was held constant. Right before expiration, the call option will still have some value, but it would steadily lose it. If the stock price were $102, and we had a call option that has a strike set at $100, the option price on the following remaining time frames: 30, 20, 10, 7, and 3 days to expiration, would be: $2.98, $2.68, $2.33, $2.21, and $2.05.

Chapter 2. Options Brokers and Simple Strategies

In order to trade successfully, you will need to access the markets. To do so, you will need the services of a broker. This is because the markets are not accessed directly by traders. Ideally, traders used to work with stockbrokers or brokerage firms. Traders would prepare their trades which would then be placed in the markets by the brokerage firms. This was the practice for many years and even decades.

Things are different today because of advances in the digital world. Online trading has become extremely common with thousands, and probably even millions of traders trading from different locations around the world. All these traders access the markets to place their trades or exit the markets via online brokers.

Digital Brokers

Today, you do not need to visit your broker at the office. All you need is a computer that is connected to the internet. With this, you are good to go. Simply find a suitable broker and begin trading. Brokers provide their clients with platforms that allow you to access the markets any time of day or night. This kind of easy access has changed the way things are done around the world. More and more people have been able to trade and generate wealth for themselves and their families.

Therefore, if you want to begin trading options, you start by identifying the best possible options broker in the market. You will then open a brokerage account with this brokerage which is an online platform. There are numerous types of brokers out there. They all have different requirements and provide a variety of tools and services.

Options trading can be tricky, sometimes difficult, and challenging. As such, you really need to ensure that you choose the correct broker. A lot of traders, even seasoned experts, are of the opinion that trading options carry a significant amount of risk especially when you begin dealing in more complex strategies.

The first step as it is you will have to find a broker that supports options trading. Not all brokerage firms support options trading so it is advisable to confirm this before proceeding. Ideally, you will have to look at about five or six different brokers and then decide which one serves your best interest. Virtually all brokers have pros and cons so try and identify one that has features that you like. These include helpful customer service, low costs, affordable fees, and fair charges, and so on.

Types of Brokers

We have different kinds of brokers. There are actually two main types. These are discount brokers and full-service brokers. A full-service broker also known as a traditional broker provides a wide variety of services to clients. These services include personalized advice to clients about where to invest or place their money. These professionals serve mostly active traders who prefer to make their own financial decisions.

On the other hand, we have discount brokers who are more suited to traders who know what they are doing and wish to manage their own affairs. As such, clients pay only a minimal amount and in return get to make most, if not all their financial decisions. What they do mostly is to execute orders from clients like you. This means that when you enter a trade or a position, the broker will execute these on your behalf.

You are also likely to encounter brokerage firms that provide a combination of these services. They generally offer a bouquet of services from which clients get to choose the services they desire. A lot of options traders, including beginners and novices, prefer the discounted services. Basically, any trader that is confident enough to trade on their own and implement options strategies is very likely to be successful.

Considerations to Keep in Mind

As a trader, when searching for a broker, you should watch out for a couple of important features. The most crucial for most traders are commission charges and great customer service. However, these should not be the only considerations. There are other important ones as well. In the end, you will have to balance out your preferences and possibly sacrifice some benefits in exchange for others.

Speed of Trades Execution and Availability

Some of the most important features that you should look out for include website availability as well as its responsiveness. There are brokers who sit on trades for so long that traders lose any benefits by losing out on timing. Speed is crucial if you are to be a profitable and successful trader.

A good platform should also be responsive. There is no need for spending so much time coming up with a strategy only for the platform to fail you. Ensure that you find a good platform that is sufficiently responsive so that you do not lose any advantages based on your analysis. Also remember to ensure that you have an excellent system from your PC or laptop computer to system, applications, and connectivity. These are crucial for a successful trading experience.

Ease of Use

Another crucial aspect of any trading platform or online brokerage is its ease of use. All too often brokerage firms will present quite complex or oblique platforms that take a while to master. Some keys may be spread apart while some functions are complex and hard to master. Such platforms are not ideal for traders.

What you need is a platform that is easy to master, user-friendly and simple features. Such a platform should also contain fantastic features that save you time and support your trades. These platforms tend to make trading easier and are much better than others. Search for trading platforms offering unitary screen order forms that cover all sorts of strategies.

Fees and Commissions

Also crucial are fees and charges including commissions, penalties, and so on. It is crucial to find an affordable broker whose costs and charges are minimal. If you are not careful, fees and charges will eat into your profits. As it is, options brokerages are super careful to stand out from the competition.

Such brokerages often charge either per contract fee or a per-trade fee. These are different in many ways. Find out exactly what fees are charged, what they cover, whether they are paid upfront and soon. Other crucial considerations include market and limit orders. Different orders will cost a different amount based on certain factors. Check the fees charged and understand exactly what is being charged.

There are sometimes hidden fees. These fees could be charged on inactive accounts, not maintaining a minimum fee in your trading account, and even a general annual account maintenance fee. Watch out for commissions that are usually charged on winnings. They do add up to significant amounts with time. Avoid platforms that charge large commissions. A low-commission broker is ideal.

Two-Way Screening

You need to know that screening should be both ways. Even as you get screened by a broker, you will need to screen them as well. Your broker will be your most crucial partner from this point on so you need to ensure that you will have a positive relationship together.

An appropriate broker is one with the necessary research and trading tools and will provide the necessary customer service, guidance, and support. This is especially important for first time traders who are new to options trading. You need also to compare and contrast other traders and see who offers you the best platform, tools, and support. This is easier nowadays because most of them have been rated by traders.

Select an Online Broker

It is important to consider the tools offered by a broker and the fees he charges. These two considerations are of paramount importance. If you are a beginner or novice trader, then you will want to find a broker who offers excellent customer service because you will definitely need some assistance along the way.

At this stage, you probably won't find brokers that charge low fees. Basically, you should aim to pay no more than $4 - $10 per trade. You probably won't trade much as a beginner and novice trader. Once your skills get better and you start trading more often, then you can consider moving to a more affordable broker.

Also, take a look at your broker's software. This software should be easy to navigate and also streamlined. A good platform that is presentable, easy to navigate and user-friendly is what you should be on the lookout for. The software should provide advice on how to access all the trading tools you will need and also access to a platform that allows you to interact with other traders.

Trading Accounts

When it comes to trade and investments, a trading account is simply an account that is held by a financial institution that you open as a trader. These accounts are not normally opened directly but via a broker or investment dealer. The account is for you and is meant for your trading and investment purposes. It can hold all sorts of securities from stocks to currencies, bonds, and numerous others.

The best way to fund your account is via your bank account. This will establish and confirm your identity. It will also prove that the funds belong to you. You cannot use a check issued by a friend to fund your account.

Margin Trading Account

You can choose between opening a margin trading account or a cash account. A margin trading account comes with a credit line directly from your broker. This credit line makes it possible for you to purchase stocks, options, and other types of securities whenever you wish. You also get the chance to buy options directly.

Cash Trading Account

This type of trading account allows you to enter trades using only the cash in your account. Basically, I you have $5,000 in your account then you can only use the $5,000 for your trades. You will also be required to close one position before acquiring more purchase power.

Since this is a cash account, you are generally not permitted to borrow any cash. The good news is that any cash settlements are often processed within a day. Let us assume you transact today. Any cash settlements can be sorted out within a 24 hour period. However, this is just with some brokers and not all. There are those who take up to 3 days to process settlements.

Margin

A lot of the time brokerage firms will offer you some margin. This is additional credit that enables you to invest in more stock. A margin account is similar to receiving a loan from an institution. This means that you will pay some interest on the cash advance. This interest is charged only if you hold a position overnight. The amount of interest charged is often 2% over and above the prevailing market rates. Remember that you will be responsible for paying back this money, regardless of whether or not you earned a profit.

Margin is often handed out to qualifying accounts at a rate of 2:1. This applies to accounts whose balance is less than $25,000. For instance, if your account balance is $15,000, then you have access to a total of $30,000 which you can use to place trades and buy into positions. For account holders with more than $25,000 then you can get access to credit in the ratio of 4:1. This is a lot of money so please be careful if and when you do qualify.

Chapter 3. The Steps Needed to Start Day Trading Options

Now that we know a little bit more about day trading options, it is time to take a look at some of the steps that you should take in order to get started. Jumping into the market may seem like a big deal, and you may be uncertain of the right steps that will make this happen. Some of the steps that are needed to start your day trading journey will include:

Pick out the capital

When you are ready to enter into your trade, you will need to have a set amount of capital ready to invest. You could trade on the margin, which is where the broker will lend you some money so you can make bigger trades, but this is incredibly risky in day trading, and as a beginner, it is not recommended for you to do this at all. The best bet, to ensure that you are going to make smart trading decisions, without increasing your risks, is just to use your own money for each trade.

Before you start trading, and while you are researching, consider setting up a savings account and adding a little money to it each month. Then use this money for your trades. This way, you know exactly how much you must spend, and you aren't guessing or trying to come up with money that you don't have later when your trade doesn't turn out the way that you want it.

Your broker will require that you add the money to the account when you are ready to start trading, so make sure it is ready to go. You can also add some extra to the account to start so that it is ready to go any time that you see a potentially good trade that you want to get in on. Once you earn some profits, you can then withdraw them into another account of your choice.

Choose a broker

One of the most important decisions you are going to make when you first get started with day trading is picking out a broker. This will determine the types of securities you can trade (for example, many brokers aren't going to work with cryptocurrencies for trading), how much you pay for each of your trades, and what kind of platform you get to use. Picking out a reputable broker, someone who is easy to work with can make a big difference in the results you can get with your trades.

The biggest thing to consider when you work with a broker, after determining that they do trade in the securities you are interested in, is their compensation plan. You want to check this out to see if it is going to be beneficial to you and your trading method. Since day trading requires a lot of small transactions during the day, you don't want to end with a compensation plan where the broker gets a set fee every time you execute a trade.

There are a lot of different fee structures that your broker can choose, and you need to learn and agree to the one that makes the most sense to you. Going with a set fee for the whole year would be ideal, but you can also work it out that you pay a percentage of your earnings, so if you don't earn anything on a trade, you won't be missing out. No matter which broker you decide to go with though, make sure to discuss the fee structure with them from the very beginning.

Learn about the market

As a beginner, it is probably best to pick maybe a handful of securities to work with. And don't work with all of them on the same day. Have a rotation, so if one security isn't doing well on a particular day, you can check out the others and use them for investing instead.

You need to learn as much about the market for that security as possible. Pull out charts on that particular security, looking at how it has done today and on a daily basis, over the past few weeks, and even over a few months or a few years. While day trading only takes place within one day, it is still a good idea to look at larger ranges to get a good idea of how the stock has performed in the past, and how it is likely to perform in the future.

We will take some time to explore more about these analyses, but you may find that working with fundamental analysis and a technical analysis at this time can really help you make smart decisions with investing. First is the technical analysis. This is basically what we already talked about where you will spend time looking over the charts, the history of how the security has performed, and information about the market, and then base your investment decision on that information.

Another option you can use when learning about the market is known as a fundamental analysis. With this method, you are going to look a bit further than the numbers on the page. You will look at who runs the company, what products the company sells, how long the company has been in business, the amount of debt to income they have, and more. To some investors, knowing these things makes it easier for them to decide whether or not they want to invest in a company.

Take advantage of all the tools that you can get your hands on. Use the charts, find some reputable news organizations, and then if your broker is able to provide some additional materials, make sure that you use these too. While you won't want to spend months looking over the charts because then you will miss some great trades (and the market is constantly changing anyway to spending too much time can leave you behind), getting a good overall understanding of your chosen securities can make trading easier later on.

Experiment a little

In some cases, your broker may be willing to give you a trial run on the platform that they use. If you are given this opportunity, then take it. This not only helps you to get familiar with the platform and see if you like it, but it also allows you to do a few sample trades and see how you would fair if you were using real money. You could execute a few trades and figure out what you need to work on, maybe see if one or two strategies work for you, and more.

Now, not all brokers are going to offer this kind of service to their customers. If it isn't offered, there are still chances for you to play with the market and see what will happen. You can pick a stock or two that you would be interested in, and then pretend that you invested. Follow the stock, using the strategy that you choose, and then see how the trade would go.

This can help you in a few ways. First, it gives you the chance to watch the market and try out a few trades, before you have to put your actual money into the investment. Yes, you may miss out on some good trades that may have made you some profit. But this is a time for learning, and it can protect you from some bad trades as you get more familiar with the market.

Once you have had a chance to do a few trades, you can then enter the market. You have a bit of experience behind you and maybe even more caution with the trades because you know that, after the experiment, a few of your trades wouldn't have gone as well as you had thought.

Decide your entry and exit points

When you enter into the stock market, especially with day trading. You must have a strategy from the very beginning. If you just go in with the idea that you want to make money (which is a given because who wants to go into day trading or any other type of trading and lose money?), and nothing else planned out, you are going to end up losing a ton of money very quickly.

Having a plan to enter the market makes things work out well because you will enter at the time that provides you with the highest potential for profits. Many people like to look at the moving averages of the security and then when they see that the security gets under this point, they will enter the market. This allows you to get the security for a discount compared to normal, and increases your chances of earning any profit, while also increase how much potential profit you can earn.

While picking an entry point may make sense, many people wonder why they need to spend their time coming up with an exit strategy as well. Shouldn't you stay in the market as long as possible and get as much as you can? The problem here is that the market with day trading is going to be very versatile and there will be a lot of ups and downs that come with it. If you aren't careful about it, and you don't make a plan, you may end up losing more money than gaining.

If you were able to enter into the market below the moving average, then your exit point should be either when the security reaches the moving average, or slightly above this point. Only set the exit strategy above this point if you have plenty of evidence to prove that it will actually get there. Then, as soon as the market moves up to that point, then you can end the trade and enjoy the benefits of your profits.

It is also a good idea to set an exit strategy in case your trades don't go the way that you want. While everyone hopes that they do a good trade and see profits, even the best traders are going to run into troubles sometimes. The market doesn't always react the way that we would like, and it may go down, even when the signs were all pointing up. Without a good exit strategy in place, it is easy to make mistakes with the trading and then stay in the market too long, resulting in a lot of lost profits. Set a small exit point on this one so that if you do lose money, at least it is only a little bit. Overall, if you are careful with your trading, hopefully you won't have to use this. But it can really help to protect your investment, and you can always re-enter the market later if you find it steadies out later in the day.

Getting started in day trading options doesn't have to be a difficult task. There are a lot of people who like to get started with day trading, and they have high hopes that they will be able to see a lot of profits with the work that they put in. If they are able to get started with the right steps, and really know how day trading works, then they will be able to get started and see amazing results.

Chapter 4. Technical Analysis

Professional traders often use a set of tools known as technical analysis in order to help them make better trades. Specifically, technical analysis can help you detect developing trend reversals in stock charts, and this information can help you get into and out of your trades at the best possible time. Technical analysis is a favorite tool of day and swing traders, and some options traders use it, but not all options traders do. Nonetheless, you should have some familiarity with it to determine if it is something you feel could help your trading.

Technical analysis involves a wide range of tools. These include looking at moving averages and specialized types of charts known as candlestick charts. Some traders also look for stock chart patterns that can signify a trend reversal, or change in price momentum.

It's important not to get too enamored with technical analysis. That is, you don't want to get into a mindset where you view technical analysis as "fact", because the cold truth about technical analysis is that it is a tool and nothing more. It is too easy to put far too much faith into technical analysis that really isn't deserved. Nonetheless, technical analysis is definitely a useful tool, and you can pick and choose specific tools of the trade that you feel will help you make more educated trading decisions.

Studying Trends with Moving Averages

The most important thing on a stock chart that a trader is going to look for on a stock chart is a trend reversal. If you are looking to profit from call options, then what you are going to look for is a relatively low stock price, or a stock price that is in decline, and then wait for it to show signs of a reversal. In other words, this is going to help you buy low, and sell high. So, the technique once you have entered a position is to study the charts looking for the coming reversal once the price has peaked, and so you can exit your position.

Moving averages are the easiest tools to use for this purpose. What a moving average does is it takes several time periods of stock data, and at each point, it calculates the average, out to a fixed number of points. The definition of a "point" is up to the individual trader, it could be an hour, a four-hour period, a day, or a week. It could even be five-minute intervals. If you are planning on trading an option over a 30 day period, then you will probably be looking at using days for your time frame. In that case, a 9-period moving average would calculate the average of the closing price at each day, using the past nine days to do the calculation.

In order to spot trend reversals, traders rely on using moving averages with different periods (but they will use the same definition of period, be it day, week, or five minutes). So, you could use a 9-period moving average, and a 20-period moving average. Alternatively, you might use a 50-period moving average, and a 200-period moving average.

Obviously a longer-period moving average is going to give you more information on the historical pricing level of the stock in question. Different types of moving averages are going to treat this in different ways. A simple moving average will do a standard mathematical average of all data points. So, if we had a 9-period simple moving average for closing prices of Apple, on a particular day it might calculate:

SMA = (212.41 + 213.11 + 212.50 +214.29 + 215.72 +216.01 + 217.22 + 217.50 + 216.95)/9

Many traders are completely content to use the simple moving average, but if you look at how it's calculated, you should note that all prices are treated the same. This is objectionable, because if you are looking to make a trade, recent prices are going to be more important to you than historical, older prices. We certainly want information from the historical pricing level of the stock, but it is more recent prices that are going to have the most impact on our trading decisions. For this reason, many traders use weighted moving averages that give more weight to recent closing prices and less weight to closing prices in the past. There are two very popular weighted moving averages that are used, the Hull moving average, and the more popular exponential moving average.

In order to detect a trend reversal, you will use two moving averages on your stock chart of the same type, but with different period lengths. So, you can use a nine day period exponential moving average with a 20-day period exponential moving average. No matter what type you choose and what periods you use, there are only two rules you need to worry about.

The first rule is known as a golden cross. This happens when the short-period moving average curve crosses above the long-period moving average curve. This tells you that the stock is likely to be entering an upward trend. In the example below, a 50-day simple moving average and a 200-day simple moving average are used. Notice that after the golden cross (the 50-day moving average crossing above the 200-day moving average), the stock enters into a relatively long-term upward trend.

The beauty of this tool is that it is very simple to use – it is also something that a beginning trader can understand quite easily.

Of course, stocks are not always going up, otherwise everyone would be rich. So, we have to know how to spot the development of a downward trend in prices as well. This is indicated by a so-called death cross. In a death cross, the short-period moving average curve crosses below the long-period moving average curve.

This is clearly illustrated in the chart below, which shows a death cross for Facebook, and the drop in stock prices that followed:

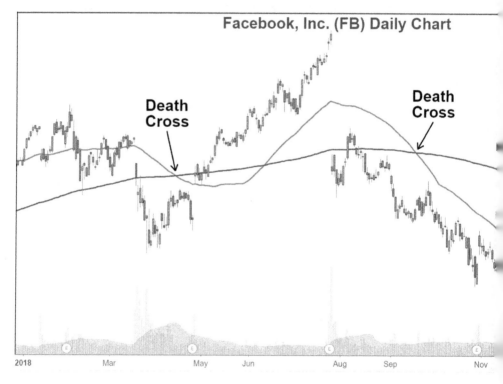

The question now is how to use crosses of moving average curves with options trading. You should see from the examples that it's actually quite simple. When you are looking to get into a trade, you should add the appropriate moving averages to your charts, and then use a golden cross or a death cross as a signal to enter or exit trades.

For call options, you want to enter a trade when there is a golden cross. Then, when the chart shows a death cross, exit your positions. It's that simple.

For put options, you will do the opposite. That is, you will wait to enter your trade until you see a death cross. For options traders, since you can profit either way, a "death" cross is also a signal for profits, but with using put options. Then you hold your position until you've either reached a level of profit you are comfortable with or you see a golden cross, indicating a coming trend reversal.

Remember that with options, the expiration date and time decay are always lurking in the background, so you don't necessarily want to wait for another crossing to occur before exiting your positions. Each case will have to be evaluated individually.

Momentum

One of the most important concepts that stock traders look for is momentum. Price momentum occurs when a large number of traders are either buying or selling a stock, pushing prices strongly in one direction or another. The tool that you can use to study the momentum of a stock price is called the Relative Strength Indicator. You can add this to your stock charts to help you study the best times to get into and out of positions to maximize possible profits.

The relative strength indicator will be displayed below your stock chart. It is a curve that can go between 0 to 100. Typically, the values 0-30 and 70-100 are what traders are looking for on the chart. When the curve goes into the range of 0-30, this means that a stock is "oversold". That is, traders have sold off too many shares, pushing prices down to a level that makes it likely that new traders are going to find the stock now an attractive buy, and so they are likely to start loading up on the stock and pushing prices upward again. The lower the RSI gets, the stronger this signal is.

On the other hand, if the RSI goes into the range of 70 and above, this indicates overbought conditions. In this case, frantic purchasing of the shares has pushed prices up too high, and traders are likely to start getting out of the stock, because they want to get out before the price drops when there is a large selloff.

The RSI should not be taken in isolation. A good way to use it is to use it in conjunction with the moving averages. So, if you see oversold conditions with the RSI, together with a golden cross, that indicates that stock prices are likely to start moving upwards. On the other hand, if the RSI indicates overbought conditions, and you also see a death cross, this can be taken as an indication that stock prices are likely to be pushed in a downward direction in the near future.

An example chart with the RSI is shown below.

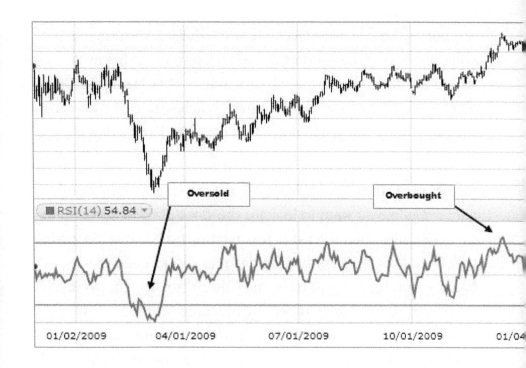

Support and Resistance

The concepts of support and resistance are important for options traders to understand, especially if you are interested in trading iron condors. These concepts are not complicated, so most readers will have no problem grasping them.

In many cases, a stock is not going to be shooting up or crashing to the floor. In fact, over most time periods of the stock market, stocks are going to be bouncing around in the same price range, and possibly gradually increasing or maybe decreasing, but over relatively short time periods staying basically the same. When this happens, we say that the stock is "ranging". The values that the stock prices range between are called support and resistance.

Support is the low price level. So, while the stock is ranging, it will dip down to the support price level, but not go below it. After it drops to support it will probably start rising again. You want to look for a price that the stock reaches at least twice over the time frame you are looking at in order to declare that a support price.

Resistance is the upper price level that the stock cannot break above. Again, you want to look for the stock price to move up to the resistance price at least twice, over the time frame. So, while the stock is ranging, it will drop down to support and then bounce around, go up to resistance, then drop back down to support again, and keep repeating this process. Stocks can actually do this for extended time periods. For options traders, when the price drops to resistance, this is a time for those trading call options to enter their positions. Put option traders would sell their positions at this point. When the price goes up to resistance level, then traders investing in call options should sell their positions, while this is a point that you would be looking to enter a position if you were interested in trading put options. The rules are basically pretty simple.

The chart below shows a stock that enters a ranging period, with support and resistance.

Chapter 5. Strategies for Options Trading

The misconception about Options Trading is that it is very difficult to understand, but that is simply not the case. Using options trading an investor can generate great amounts of profits from small initial investments with minimum risks. Options are powerful and flexible and can prove to be extremely beneficial if properly used. The way to do that is to gain knowledge about the working and fundamentals of options trading before starting the actual trade.

Covered Call

The covered call strategy generates profits through the means of premiums. There's a term called "Long" for covered call. This term is used to denote the purchase of assets with the optimism that the value of said asset would rise in the future. Selling call option on this long position enables the investors to generate recurring incomes. Covered calls are neutral in nature and it is estimated that for the duration of call option on an asset, the price of the asset will change only minutely, be it high or low. Covered calls are also known as buy-write. Although covered calls provide generous income on short terms, with some patience it can help the investors to generate income as a chain of premiums. If the investor is willing to wait out, they can choose to keep the underlying assets and not sell them even in the case of a small depression, elevation or inactivity, this works as a protection scheme on long asset position and generate income in premiums. A disadvantage is that if the price of the underlying stock exceeds the price of the option, then the investor has to give up the gains on stocks.

Covered call being a neutral strategy means it is not optimal for investors who are very brutish in terms of earning. It is suggested that such investors keep the stock on hold and not exercise the write option as if the asset price goes up; the option takes the profit on the asset. Also, if the stocks take a big hit and the estimated loss is going to be too great for recovery from premiums using the call option, the investor should sell the stocks.

Two terms are used for keeping track of profit and loss in this strategy, these terms are:

The maximum loss- It is calculated by removing the amount received as premium from the purchasing price of the underlying asset.

The maximum profit- it is calculated by calculating the total of strike price of short call option and premium received and then subtracting the purchasing price from it.

Married Put

Married put acts like a safety net in the field of options trading. The investor who is holding a long position has to purchase the at-the-money put option to prevent themselves from taking a big hit if the stock prices fall.

Married put is also known as synthetic long call. Some people may think married put to be similar to covered put, but that is not the case. Married put is optimal for those bullish investors who are wary of probable loss in near-sightedness. Another benefit of implementing the put option is that with this option, the investor gets to enjoy the benefits exclusively available to stockowners such as voting rights and receiving dividends. So is not the case if the investor has invested in a call only option. Same as the covered put, married put strategy can allow the investors to reap unlimited benefits generated from the initial investment in the underlying stocks. The only deductions from the profit will be the investment used for buying premium of the put option. There's a stage called breakeven at which the price of the underlying asset exceeds the price paid for the options premium. It is after this stage that the profit begins to generate.

Another new term called Floor is used, which is referred to the difference between the actual price at which the underlying stock was purchased, and the strike price of the put.

The exercise of a put options falls under the category of married put only when both the assets and the put option is purchased on the same day. The broker is then informed to deliver the bought stocks when the investor exercises their put option.

The question that now arises is when to use this strategy?

As mentioned in the first line of this concept, married put acts like a safety net or insurance for the investors and that is how it should be addressed, not as a money-reaping strategy. The price paid for purchasing premium of put is dedicated from the total profits. This strategy should be used to act as a protection of stocks for short terms so as to counter the probable dip in the stock prices. This gives the investor some sort of reassurance knowing that the chances of loss have been diminished and they can continue to trade.

Bull Call Spread

Bull Call Spread is ideal for use when a hike in the price of the underlying stock is estimated in the near future by the investor. In Bull Call Spread, the investor has to purchase two specific call options on the same underlying asset and within the month of contract expiration. These two call options are at-the-money call option and out-of-the-money call option. Upon beginning the trade, the Bull Call Spread takes a debit from their account, which is known as bull call debit spread.

The cost of implementing bullish options of the trade is eliminated by the sale of out-of-the-money call option.

The total profit is calculated by taking the difference between the strike price of the call options and the bull call debit that was taken at the beginning of the trade.

Similarly, the maximum loss is calculated by the addition of all the costs incurred in the form of commissions and premiums. An investor faces maximum loss when the prices of the underlying assets fall near to the date of expiration and is either less than or equal to the higher strike price of the two calls.

A few terms are associated with Bull Call Spread, which are as follows:

Break-even point: In the Bull Call Spread, The breakeven point is calculated by the addition of prices of the total premiums purchased and the strike price of the long call.

Intense Bull Call Spread: Intense Bull Call Spread is determined by subtracting the lower strike price of two call options from the higher one. The investor can reap maximum profits only when the stock prices elevate by a significant margin.

What makes Bull Call Spread alluring to the traders?

There are a number of advantages of the Bull Call Spread strategy that attract the options traders. These advantages are-

A)   There is a certain limit to the loss. Bull Call Spread prevents the investors from facing too huge losses.

B)   Bull Call Spread generates higher returns from the initial investment than other strategies in which only call options are purchased.

C)   Call options can be bought at a lower price than the strike price.

What are the downsides of Bull Call Spread?

Since Bull Call spread generates more profits than the strategies in which only call options are bought, it means there are more purchases in this strategy than other strategies which means cost paid as the commission is higher. Bull Call Spread generates no profits if the price of the underlying asset exceeds the price of the out-of-the-money call option.

What additional steps can you take in Bull Call Spread to strengthen your position?

A)   When the prices of the underlying assets are speculated to elevate above the strike price of the short call option, the investor can choose to implement the buy to close option on the out-of-the-money short call and then short it to establish another out-of-the-money call again. Another alternative to that is the investor may just exercise buy to close on the out-of-the-money short call option and leave it at that to reap benefits from the long call option.

B) In a situation where the prices of the underlying assets are not expected to change majorly, the investor can implement an out-of-the-money call option at a higher strike price, this transitions the Bull Call spread position to Long Call Ladder spread and the break-even point is decreased.

C) The investor can also transition into Bear Call Spread by closing the long call option. This is ideal for when the price of the underlying stock is speculated to turn back upon reaching the strike price of the short call. The transition has to be done as soon as the price of the underlying stocks becomes equal to the price of short call.

Bear Put Spread

This strategy is adopted in the situations where a drop in the price of the underlying asset is expected. Bear Put Spread consists of buying put options at a specific strike price and selling an equal number of puts at a lower strike price which share the same expiration date.

Two components make up the Bear Put Spread which are-

A) A short put having a low strike price.

B) A long put having a higher strike price.

Both of the puts share the same underlying assets and same expiration date. In the Bear Put, profits are achieved where there is a depression in the underlying stock prices.

These two components affect the profit and losses in these ways:

A)   It limits the profits when the strike price of the short put having a lower strike price is higher than the price of the underlying stock.

B)   It limits the loss when the strike price of the long put having a higher strike price is lower than that of the underlying stock.

Additions steps that can be taken for Bear Put Spread to strengthen your position

A)   When the price of the underlying stock is expected to fall below the price of short put having a lower strike price, the investor is suggested to implement the buy to close the short put option and in return sell it to buy an out-of-the-money put option. Similar to Bull Call spread, the investor can opt for an alternative where he just implements buy to close on short put option and keep the long put as it is to reap the profits.

B)   If a halt or a moderate drop is expected in the price of the underlying stock when it becomes equal to the price of the underlying stock, the investor can transition to Bull Put Spread by closing out of the Long Put option and purchase out-of-the-money put options.

What makes Bear Put Spread appealing to the investors?

There are a number of attractions that allure the investors. They are:

A)   The most appealing feature of the Bear Put Spread is that it limits the risk of loss. This reassurance convinces the investors to try it out. The total amount paid for purchasing the put options in Bear Put Spread is lower than the price of a single put purchased independently because the capital spent for purchasing the long put option having higher strike price is compensated from the sale of the short put option having a lower strike price.

Chapter 6. Strangles and Straddles

Options allow you to create strategies that simply are not possible when investing in stocks. There are two ways that you can do this, they are known as strangles and straddles. This is a more complex strategy than simply buying a long call option or a long put. But it's not really that complicated, you just have to understand some basics on how to set them up in order to make a profit.

The strategy that is used in this case is dependent on a large move by the stock. There are many situations where this might be appropriate. But mainly, this is something you will consider using when you are looking to profit from an earnings call.

Earnings calls cause major price shifts in the big stocks. The price shift is largely determined by what the analysts "expectations" are for earnings, and so this is not always a rational process. If the company beats the analyst expectations when it comes to earnings per share, this creates a positive "surprise" that will usually send the stock soaring. The amount of "surprise" is given by the percentage difference between the actual value and the expected value. So, in this case, if you had bought a call option, you could make amazing levels of profit from the option by selling it in the next day or two, as long as the new higher price level is maintained.

But the problem is, you have no idea beforehand whether the earnings are going to exceed or fail to meet the analyst expectations. The silly thing about this (from a common-sense perspective) is that even if the company is profitable, if they fail to meet analyst expectations, these results in massive disappointment. So you might see share prices drop from a sell-off even if the company is profitable. This is "surprise" in a negative way.

The impact of failing to meet expectations can be magnified if the company also has some bad news to share. This news hit Netflix stock hard, it dropped by a walloping $42. If you had purchased a put option, that could have meant a $4000 profit.

The problem is that you don't know ahead of time which way the stock is going to go. It's one thing to look back and say well you could have had a put option and made $4k in a day, but often companies reveal information in earnings calls that have been under wraps. Nobody had any inkling that Netflix was going to be losing subscribers until the earnings call.

Second, analyst expectations are somewhat arbitrary. Defining success or failure in terms of them is actually pretty silly, but that is the way things work right now. But the point is it's really impossible to know whether or not these arbitrary expectations are met prior to the earnings call. It's also impossible to gauge the level of reaction that is going to be seen from exceeding or failing to meet expectations.

Since we don't know which way the stock is going to move, it would seem that a good strategy to use is to buy a call and a put at the same time. That is precisely the idea behind a straddle and strangle.

That way, you profit no matter what happens, as long as the price on the market changes fairly strongly in one direction or another. When you set up a straddle or strangle, there is a middle "red zone" that bounds the current share price over which you are going to lose money. But if the share price either goes above the boundaries of this zone or below it, you will make profits.

If the stock shoots upward, this means that the put option is going to drop massively in value. So, it's basically a write off for you. But if the stock makes a strong move, as they often do after positive earnings calls, you stand to make enough profits from the call option that was a part of your trade to more than make up for the loss of the put. The potential upside gain is in theory unlimited. Of course, in practice, share prices don't rise without limit, but they might rise, $10, $20, or $40, and that could potentially earn profits of roughly $1,000-$4,000, more than covering any loss from the now worthless put option.

The opposite situation applies as well. If the stock drops by a large amount, you make profits. Profits to the downside are capped because a stock price cannot decline below zero. That said, if the stock drops by a significant amount, you can still make hundreds to thousands of dollars per contract virtually overnight.

Doing this requires some attention on your part. You are going to have to think ahead in order to implement this strategy and profit from it. Remember that you can use a straddle or strangle any time that you think the stock is going to make a major shift one way or the other. An example of a non-earning season situation, where this could be a useful strategy, would be a new product announcement. Think Apple. If Apple is having one of their big presentations, if the new phone that comes out disappoints the analysts, share prices are probably going to drop by a large amount. On the other hand, if it ends up surprising viewers with a lot of new features that make it the must-have phone again, this would send Apple stock soaring.

The problem here is you really don't know which way it's going to go. There are going to be leaks and rumors, but basing your trading decisions on that is probably not a good approach, often, the rumors are wrong. A strangle or straddle allows you to avoid that kind of situation and make money either way.

Other situations that could make this useful include changes in management or any political interaction. We mentioned the government recently made a privacy settlement with Facebook. If you knew when the settlement was going to occur but wasn't sure what it was going to be, using strangle or straddle might be a good way to earn money from the large price moves that were sure to follow.

The same events that might warrant buying a long call such as a GDP number or jobs report, for options on index funds, are also appropriate for strangles and straddles.

Implied Volatility Strategy

Implied volatility is very important when a big event like an earnings report is coming. This gives you a way to make profits. In fact, we are going to call this the implied volatility strategy.

Remember, implied volatility is a projection of what the volatility of the stock is going to be in the near future. When there is an earnings call, the volatility is going to be extreme on the day after the call. Therefore, you are going to see the implied volatility growing as earnings day approaches.

At the time I am writing this, it is 24 hours before Facebook's earnings call. The implied volatility is 74%, which is very high. In contrast, for Apple, which is more than a week away from its next earnings call, the implied volatility is only 34%. This is for a $207.50 strike put, with a share price of $207.9.

The strategy is to profit from the implied volatility. You want to enter your position one to two weeks before the earnings call or big announcement. As implied volatility increases, this is going to swamp out time decay and cause a big rise in the option price.

Using that Apple put option, if we assumed that there were only 4 days to expiration, but the implied volatility had risen to about where Facebook is and there were no other changes (so we will leave the share price where it was), the price of the put option would increase by about $330.

So if nothing else, you could profit from the change of implied volatility. It will probably go highest the day before the earnings call.

This is going to be magnified if you trade a strangle or straddle. Prior to the earnings call, both the put and the call option are going to increase a great deal in value because of implied volatility. So you could sell the strangle the day before the earnings call and book some profits then. Since a strangle or straddle can earn big profits if there is a large move in the share price, you won't find any problems locating a buyer.

Estimating Price from Implied Volatility

If you know the implied volatility, you can make an estimate of the price range of the stock. This can be done using a simple formula.

(Stock price x implied volatility)/SQRT (days in a year)

If you don't want to do the calculation, if we take the square root of 365, it is about 19.1. For example, we use Facebook with a share price of $202.50 and an implied volatility of 76%.

Facebook	
Stock Price	$202.50
Implied Vol.	0.76
Days in a year	19.1049732
Expected Change	$8.06
Upper Range	$210.56
Lower Range	$194.44

The implied volatility gives us an idea of what traders are thinking, in regard to the upcoming earnings call, but of course, we can never be sure what is really going to happen until it does. But this gives us upper and lower bounds. Using the information that we have available, we can guess that Facebook might rise to $210.56 a share after the earnings call, or it might drop to $194.44 per share after the earnings call. You can use these boundaries to set up your strategy. However, remember that if there is a big surprise, it can go well past these boundary points in one direction or the other.

What is a Long Straddle?

To set up a straddle, you buy a put option and a call option simultaneously (buy = take a long position). The maximum loss that you can incur is the sum of the cost to buy the call option plus the sum of the cost to buy the put option. This loss is incurred when you enter the trade.

With a straddle, you buy a call option and a put option together. And they would be with the same strike price. By necessity, this means that one option is going to be in the money and one option is going to be out of the money. When approaching an earnings call, the prices can be kind of steep, because you want to price them close to the current share price. That way, it gives us some room to profit either way the stock price moves.

A maximum loss is only incurred if you hold the position to expiration. You can always choose to sell it early, if it looks like it's not going to work out, and take a loss that is less than the maximum.

Chapter 7. Risk Management

Excellent risk management can save the worst trading strategy, but horrible risk management will sink even the best strategy. This is a lesson that many traders learn painfully over time, and I suggest you learn this by heart and install it deep within you even if you can't fully comprehend that statement.

Risk management has many different elements to both quantitative and qualitative. When it comes to options trading, the quantitative side is minimal thanks to the nature of options limiting risk by themselves. However, the qualitative side deserves a lot of attention.

Risk

So what is risk anyway? Logically, it is the probability of you losing all of your money. In trading terms, you can think of it as being the probability of your actions putting you on a path to losing all of your capital. A good way to think about the need for good risk management is to ask you what a bad trader would do? Forget trading, what would a bad business person do with their capital?

Well, they would spend it on useless stuff that adds nothing to the bottom line. They would also increase expenses, market poorly, not take care of their employees, and be in disciplined with regards to their processes. While trading, you don't have employees or marketing needs, so you don't need to worry about that.

Do you have suppliers and costs? Well, yes, you do. Your supplier is your broker, and you pay fees to execute your trades.

That is the cost of access. In directional trading, you have high costs as well because taking losses is a necessary part of trading. With market neutral or non-directional trading, your losses are going to be minimal, but you should still seek to minimize them.

What about discipline? Do you think you can trade and analyze the market well if you've just returned home from your job and are tired? If you didn't sleep properly last night? Or if you've argued with your spouse or partner? The point I'm making is that the more you behave like a terrible business owner, the more you increase your risk of failure.

Odds and Averages

Trading requires you to think a bit differently about profitability. I spoke about minimizing costs, and your first thought must have been to seek to reduce losses and maximize wins. This is a natural product of linear or ordered thinking. The market, however, is chaotic and linear thinking is going to get you nowhere.

Instead, you need to think in terms of averages and odds. Averages imply that you need to worry about your average loss size and your average win size. Seek to decrease the former and increase the latter. Notice that when we talk about averages, we're not necessarily talking about reducing the total number of losses. You can reduce the average by either reducing the sum of your losses or by increasing the number of losing trades while keeping the sum of the losses constant. This is a shift in thinking you must make.

Thinking in this way sets you up nicely to think in terms of odds, because in chaotic systems all you can bank on are odds playing out in the long run. For example, if you flip a coin, do you know in advance whether it's going to be a heads or tails? Probably not. But if someone asked you to predict the distribution of heads versus tails over 10,000 flips, you could reasonably guess that it'll be 5000 heads and 5000 tails. You might be off by a few flips either way, but you'll be pretty close percentage-wise.

In fact, the greater the number of flips, the lesser your error percentage. This is because the odds inherent in a pattern that occurs in a chaotic system express themselves best over the long run. Your trading strategy is precisely such a pattern. The market is a chaotic system. Hence, you should focus on executing your strategy as it is meant to be executed over and over again and worry about profitability only in the long run.

Contrast this with the usual attitude of traders who seek to win every single trade. This is impossible to accomplish since no trading strategy or pattern is correct 100% of the time. If we were discussing directional strategies, I'd spend a lot more time on this, but the fact is that options take care of a lot of this ambiguity themselves.

This is because you don't have to do much when trading options. You enter and then monitor the trade. Sure, it helps to have some directional bias, but even if you get it wrong, your losses will be extremely limited, and you're more likely to hit winners than losers.

Despite this, always think of your strategy in terms of its odds. There are two basic metrics to measure this. The first is the win rate of your system. This is simply the percentage of winners you have. The second is your payout ratio which is the average wins size divided by the average loss size.

Together these two metrics will determine how profitable your system is. Both of them play off one another, and an increase in one is usually met by a decrease in another. It takes an extremely skillful trader to increase both simultaneously.

Risk per Trade

The quantitative side of risk management when it comes to options trading is lesser than what you need to take care of when trading directionally. However, this doesn't mean there's nothing to worry about. Perhaps the most important metric of them all is your risk per trade. The risk per trade is what ultimately governs your profitability.

How much should you risk per trade? Common wisdom says that you should restrict this to 2% of your capital. For options trading purposes, this is perfectly fine. In fact, once you build your skill and can see opportunities better, I'd suggest increasing it to a higher level.

A point that you must understand here is that you must keep your risk per trade consistent for it to have any effect. You might see a wonderful setup and think that it has no chance of failure, but the truth is that you don't know how things will turn out. Even the prettiest setup has every chance of failing, and the ugliest setup you can think of may result in a profit. So never adjust your position size based on how something looks.

Calculating your position size for a trade is a pretty straightforward task. Every option's strategy will have a fixed maximum risk amount. Divide the capital risk by this amount, and that gives you your position size. Round that down to the nearest whole number since you can only buy whole number lots when it comes to contract sizes.

For example, let's say your maximum risk is $50 per lot on the trade. Your capital is $10,000. Your risk per trade is 2%. So the amount you're risking on that trade is 2% of 10,000 which is $200. Divide this by 50, and you get 4. Hence, your position size is four contracts or 400 shares. (You'll buy the contracts, not the shares.)

Why is it important to keep your risk per trade consistent? Well, recall that your average win and loss size is important when it comes to determining your profitability. These, in conjunction with your strategy's success rate, determine how much money you'll make. If you keep shifting your risk amount per trade, you'll shift your win and loss sizes. You might argue that since it's an average, you can always adjust amounts to reflect an average.

My counter to that is how would you know which trades to adjust in advance? You won't know which ones are going to be a win or a loss, so you won't know which trade sizes to adjust to meet the average. Hence, keep it consistent across all trades and let the math work for you.

Aside from risk per trade, there are some simple metrics you should keep track of as part of your quantitative risk management plan.

Drawdown

A drawdown refers to the reduction in capital your account experiences. Drawdowns by themselves always occur. The metrics you should be measuring are the maximum drawdown and recovery period. If you think of your account's balance as a curve, the maximum drawdown is the biggest peak to trough distance in dollars. The recovery period is the subsequent time it took for your account to make new equity high.

If your risk per trade is far too high, your max drawdown will be unacceptably high. For example, if you risk 10% per trade and lose two in a row, which is very likely, your drawdown is going to be 20%. This is an absurdly large hole to dig your way out. Consider that your capital has decreased by 20% and the subsequent climb back up needs to be done on lesser capital than previously.

This is why you need to keep your risk per trade low and in line with your strategy's success rate. The best way to manage drawdowns and limit the damage they cause is to put in place risk limits per day, week, and month. Even professional athletes who train to do one thing all the time have bad days, so it's unfair to expect yourself to be at 100% all the time.

These risk limits will take you out of the game when you're playing poorly. A daily risk limit is to prevent you from getting into a spiral of revenge trading. A good limit to stick to when starting off is to stop trading if you experience three losses in a row. This is pretty unlikely with options trades to be honest unless you screw up badly, but it's good to have a limit in place from a perspective of discipline.

Next, aim for a maximum weekly drawdown limit of 5% and a monthly drawdown limit of 6-8%. These are pretty high limits, to be honest, and if you are a directional trader, these limits do not apply to you. Directional traders need to be a lot more conservative than options trader when it comes to risk.

Understand that these are hard stop limits. So if your account has hit its monthly drawdown level within the first week, you need to take the rest of the month off. Overtrading and a lack of reflection on progress can cause a lot of damage, and a drawdown is simply a reflection of that.

Chapter 8. Credit and Debit Spreads

We saw how to set up a trade that could profit no matter which way the stock moves, with a fixed loss that is set at the outset of entering the trade. We are going to look at some more advanced strategies including credit spreads. Your broker is probably going to require that you are a level 3 trader in order to implement these strategies, because they involved selling to open options without owning the share of stock or putting up the capital to cover the purchase of shares from a put option. The only capital that is required to put up in these cases is the maximum loss that might be realized from the trade.

There are four different strategies that can be put in place here, and we are going to examine each in turn. When you enter into a credit spread, this is a sell to open trade and you are looking to earn a regular income. These types of trades are not always going to go your way that is certainly true. However, they are considered to be relatively safe ways to sell premium in order to earn money. A put credit spread is somewhat equivalent to selling a naked put. You will see how that works out as we go through the details, but selling naked puts is one of the most common and profitable income strategies with options. To sell naked puts, you have to be a level 4 trader with a margin account, however. So selling a put credit spread removes the margin requirement and you can be a level 3 trader and use this strategy. The difference between a put credit spread and a naked put as far as money earned is that per trade, a put credit spread is going to earn less money than selling a naked put.

Conversely, you can sell a call credit spread as well. We will explore the reasons that you would choose to sell this instead of the put credit spread below. What you need to be aware of is that selling a put credit spread is the same bet as buying what is known by the name of call debit spread, and selling a call credit spread is the same bet as buying a put debit spread.

We are going to be betting, to a certain extent, on the directional move of the stock. However, as we will see it isn't going to matter how much the stock moves, as long as it's past the breakeven point.

The beauty of these strategies is that anyone can use them, as long as you can round up a few hundred dollars. So you can start generating income from these types of options strategies fairly quickly. We will be discussing this as well as we move along to examine each case. We will get started by looking at the put credit spread.

Put Credit Spread

The idea behind a put credit spread is to earn money from selling a put option. But in order to mitigate the risk, you buy a put option simultaneously. This is different than selling a naked put option, where you just sell one option and that is the end of it. Since the option that you buy is going to mitigate your risk a little bit, you are not held to the same standards as someone who is selling naked put options. That said, you still have to have a level 3 trading account in order to use this strategy.

The first thing to realize about the put credit spread is that you are selling to open the position. So this is selling, not buying to trade options. Theoretically, there is a risk of assignment, but as we'll see, it's not a real risk in practical terms, and because the trade is mitigated by the second put which you buy to open the trade, the practical impact of this is minimal.

The two options are bought and sold in one trade, so this is considered a single trade and is not two separate trades. You can buy a put debit spread, so the other party to the trade is doing that when you sell to open your position.

The belief that is behind this type of trade is that you are expecting the price of the stock to stay about where it is now, only minimally decrease in price, or increase in price. It is considered a "bullish" move, and so sometimes, goes by the name bull credit spread, but put credit spread is far more descriptive.

Second, it's not really a bullish move, in the sense that you are hoping that the stock price is going to increase by a lot. Certainly, you will be better off if that does indeed happen. If you set it up right, you will earn the maximum possible profit right off the bat and give some room for the stock to fall before that situation changes.

One of the unique properties of a put credit spread that we have not seen yet in our examination of options is that when the price reaches a certain level that is basically it. A further increase in share price is not going to increase our profits. In the example below, consider a put credit spread for Amazon. When you sell to open the position, you get a credit to your account of $4.92 (x 100 shares for $492 total). The share price is currently in the maximum gain zone. If the share price moved up by $100, it would have zero impact on the seller of this credit spread, other than having them breathe a sigh of relief that they are definitely going to profit from the trade.

So, it's kind of a bullish strategy, but what you are really doing with a put credit spread is you are hoping that the price doesn't fall. You are using out of the money put options to set up the trade, and the hope here is that they are going to expire out of the money and that you will pocket the net premium paid on the deal.

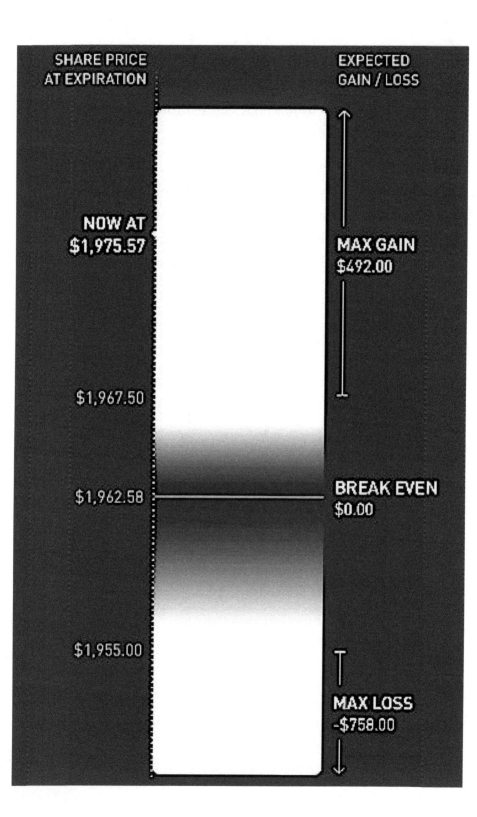

Notice that the amount of loss for the trade is capped as well. These amounts can vary considerably depending on how you set them up. In this case, the share price of Amazon is $1,975.57. The strike prices used are $1,967.50 and $1,955.00, both with the same expiration date.

Remember, these are both put options. When a put option is exercised, that means the trader who sells to open the position must buy a hundred shares of the stock. However, the price for the exchange would be at the strike price.

This can sound a little scary because, in the way that this trade is set up, you are selling a put option so could, in theory, have an obligation to buy the stock. But because of the way these are set up, you really aren't in any danger, even if the option is exercised. We will see how that works out in a little bit.

Collateral Requirements

You will notice from the figure that there is a calculated max loss. We are going to learn how to calculate the maximum loss in a little bit, but for now, let's note that this is an amount of cash you are going to need to have on hand in order to complete the trade. It's important to remember that, in this case – you are not buying anything. Consequently, the cash that you put up in order to enter the trade functions as collateral that would be used to cover your position should occur a maximum loss. So, in this case, the maximum loss is given as $758. So in order to enter the trade, we would have to deposit $758 into the account. We would, in turn, receive a credit for $492 for each contract, but that is not cash you can utilize until one of two situations happens. The first thing that would happen is that you close the position early.

In this case, we are not really worried about the options being exercised. But, the worry might be that the stock could do a dramatic move on expiration day, and by then, you can't get out of the trade. In our example, the breakeven price is $1,962.58. If Amazon suddenly dipped down to that price on expiration day, we'd end up with nothing (although if it didn't drop any further, we'd get to keep our collateral). So, you might want to buy it back and close your position before it gets to that point. This would work just like with the covered call.

As time goes on and we get closer to expiration, time decay is going to wipe out the value of these options. So, we can purchase it now at a lower price than we sold it for, and the difference would be our profit.

Let's take a look at the higher strike price, which is $1,967.50. At nine days left until the contract comes to an end, the implied volatility is 29%. The market price is $33, so the total cost for this option is $3,300. So you are selling this option. But we are focusing here on the price change, if it stays out of the money toward expiration.

Now let's fast forward to 1 day prior to expiration and estimate the price. We will assume that the implied volatility stays the same. If the share price stays the same (extremely unlikely), the put option has dropped all the way to $833. So you could buy it back and still have a profit of $2,467 (this is complicated by the fact we also bought a put option, but hold on for a moment).

But what if the price of the shares increased by $10? That would be a minor move for a stock with a share price that is that high. In that case, the value of the put is even lower, dropping to $519.

Of course, we also bought a put as a part of this transaction. The other put had a strike price of $1955. If a day before expiration the share price is up to $10, the value of this put is $247. When we close our position, we would get that back. It would help to mitigate the $519 spent to close the other position. The total hit would be around $272. So the profit would be $492-$272 = $220, in the event we bought it back under those conditions.

But if the stock price were rising, I would probably just let it expire. The idea that it would rise to $10 and then would fall back down again, and then would fall into territory that would wipe out our profits, and have this happens without any external events, strains credulity.

But every person has their own risk tolerance.

The point is the same as it was with the call options, you can mitigate your risk or you can take a chance to let the options expire and take maximum profit. What actually transpires is going to depend on the situation on the ground at the time.

Buying back your options is more important with negative puts, because of the risk of assignment. The risk with a put credit spread just isn't all that significant.

Chapter 9. Managing Options Positions

When you initially learn options, you generally find out how to practice your options. All things considered, that's what the strike cost is about. The strike cost is our activity cost. Nonetheless, as a general rule, you will find that the activity options are rarely used.

The confusing wording of shutting requests makes it hard to choose which request to use at what time, particularly without giving it much thought. We will examine when you should offer to close, buy to close or exercise your options position. This will give you the ideal approach to close your positions and lock in your benefit.

USING SELL TO CLOSE

Using sell to close and buy to close requests will generally be used often times. The contrast between the two relies upon what position you have unlocked.

When you unlatch your situation with a buy to open request, you use an offer to close request to close the position.

A buy to unlock request is used when you are buying your options, going long your position, or paying a net charge to open the position.

For instance:

If you need to buy a long put on The Option Prophet (TOP), you will use a buy to open request. This remains constant for a long call, bull call spread, bear put spread, long straddle, long choke, and so on.

You accept that TOP will have an increment in cost throughout the following month. To exploit this move, you buy to unlock 1 contract of TOP 40 Call for 2.00. TOP increases, as you anticipated, and now that call is worth 3.50. Your spot is as yet 14 days out from lapse, yet you need to feel free to close the position and lock in your benefit. You use an offer to close requests and gather $1.50 in benefit.

This is calculated thus, 3.50 − 2.00 = 1.50 benefit

Yet, what occurs if you have a long option and a short option in one position? Option systems, for example, bull call spreads and bear put spreads, have both a long option and a short option in the trade.

The ideal approach to keep track is to see how you unlocked the general trade. Bull call spreads and bear put spreads are both unlocked with buy to unlock requests. They are additionally unlatched with a net charge. Unlocking a spot with a net charge implies you are paying to unlock it. Then again, a net credit implies you are getting money to unlock the spot.

So even though the position has a short and long option within it, since you unlock it with buy to open request, and even though it is traded with a net charge, you would use an offer to close request to close the spot.

An offer to close requests can be used whenever during the life of the option. You don't need to hold up until lapse before using it. If you need to unlock a position today and use the offer to close the request tomorrow, you can.

USING BUY TO CLOSE

If an offer to close request is used when you are net-long on a position or pay a net charge, then a buy to close request is used when you are net short on a position, or when you get a net credit.

When you unlock your spot with an offer to open requests, you use a buy to close requests to close the spot.

For instance:

If you need to short an approach, The Option Prophet, you will use an offer to open request. This goes the equivalent for an iron condor, bear call spread, short put, bull put spread, short straddle, short choke, and so on.

You accept that The Option Prophet will increment in cost throughout the following month. To exploit this move, you offer 1.25 TOP increases to open 1 contract of TOP 30 Puts, as you anticipated, and now the put is worth 0.50. Your spot is as yet 14 days out from lapse, yet you need to feel free to close the position and lock in your benefit. You use a buy to close request and gather $0.75 in benefit.

This is calculated thus, 1.25 − 0.50 = 0.75 benefit

Once more, when you manage an option technique that has numerous long and short options in it, you have to consider the general position. When you exchange an iron condor, you are short two and long two options. Notwithstanding, the all-out position is traded for a net credit. When you go to close the iron condor, you will need to buy to close the position.

WHEN TO EXERCISE OPTIONS

If you offer to close after you buy to open and buy to close after you offer to open, when do you practice your options?

Practicing options are used when you need to change over your options spot into stock. Most option brokers never really need to change over their options to stock; in this manner, practicing options are seldom used.

There are times you might need to claim stock by changing over your options. To practice your options, you must make a long put or long a call.

Short options never can practice their options; short options must be allotted.

To return to our options, a long put gives you the privilege to sell the stock, and a long call gives you the privilege to buy a stock.

You now are long 1 contract of a TOP 40 call, and TOP is trading for $45. You concluded that you need to claim the TOP stock, so you practice the agreement. When you practice the agreement, you will buy 100 portions of TOP at $40 (the strike cost).

Presently, when you buy the stock, fight the temptation to go back and sell it for $45. If you plan just to buy the stock and pivot and trade them for a benefit, you would prefer not to work out. You can accomplish similar outcomes with less expense if you offer to close your position.

When we look at practicing a long put, you will sell the offers as opposed to buying the offers.

You are long 1 contract of a TOP 30 put, and TOP is trading at $25. You choose to short the stock, so you practice your agreement. When you practice the contract, you will short 100 portions of TOP at $30 (the strike cost).

Much the same as with our long call, you would prefer not to practice the agreement so you can quickly close the position and gather the profit. If that were the situation, you would offer to close your long put. This will enable you to get the profit at a lower expense.

If you need to practice your option, you should contact the option company and let them know about your expectations. A few financiers will have catches to assign that you need to practice your option. However, most businesses will have you bring in to affirm your arrangements. Most financiers are going to charge you an additional expense to practice your options.

If your options are one-penny in-the-money at lapse, it will consequently be practiced by your business. Assuming that you want to practice your options, you have to finish it off with a buy to close or offer to close requests before termination. Holding up too long could be hindering to your portfolio. You could rest on Friday with 5 entries that are marginally in-the-money and wake up Monday with 500 portions of stock in your portfolio.

DON'T EXERCISE/PRACTICE OUT OF THE MONEY OPTIONS

Never practice an option which is out-of-the-money. Practicing options are intended for in-the-money options as they were. This is conclusively clarified with a model.

You now are long a call at 50 strikes. Your fundamental is at present trading at $40, and you choose to practice. Presently you have changed over your options into offers at $50.00 even though the basic is just trading at $40; you have a loss. If you needed to get the portions of the stock, you ought to have offered to close, finished off your options and bought the offers in the market for $40 rather than $50. Try not to set yourself up by beginning with a loss, just options that are exercise in-the-money.

DON'T EXERCISE AN OPTION BEFORE EXPIRATION

When practicing your options before termination, you are giving up the properties of the options for which you've officially paid.

In the first place, you will relinquish the time price of the options. If your basic is trading at $50, and you're on a long call options at the $45 strike, you will have at any rate a $5 benefit (50 - 45). If you practice your options before the expiry, that is your lone benefit on that position.

If you have time staying before the lapse, your call will have a greater benefit without anyone else's input. The benefit of your call would be $5 + time value. When you practice, you lose the time value.

You could offer to close the options in the market for more than $5 if it is before lapse. The closer you get to lapse, the more your time worth abatements until it comes to $0. Your call would be worth $5 at termination, and that is the point at which you practice.

The second reason you don't practice before lapse is on the grounds that you will relinquish the protection options give.

You are long an approach the $30 strike that cost $3.00 and terminates in about fourteen days, and your fundamental is trading for $40. You concluded you're close enough to lapse and need to practice your call. You never again have those options and now hold 100 offers at $30. The following day an unexpected declaration is discharged that the organization is under scrutiny for misrepresentation. The stock starts to sink, and toward the day's end is worth $20. You are presently sitting on a $1,000 loss. If you had held those options, it would be useless now. However, your all-out loss would have just been $300.

Even though you will begin your options instruction finding out about practicing options at the strike value, you will find that you once in a while will practice genuine positions. Most options brokers never need to claim the stock. They trade options to deal with the agreements forward and backward.

When you buy to open, go long, or pay a net charge for a position, go long or open; you will use an offer to near close the position.

If you offer to open, go short, or get a net acknowledgment for a position, you will use a buy to near close the position.

When you manage a place that is progressively confused and has both long and short options, you will recollect how the first exchange was set up. Did you go long on the position and pay a charge, or did you go short the position and get a credit.

If you would like to practice your options, ensure your spot is in-the-money and at termination.

Never practice a situation to finish off the exchange and gather the benefit. You will get a similar outcome for less expense if you use a buy to close or offer to close requests.

Chapter 10.   Winning Tricks for Options Trading

Financial freedom can be depicted in the number of profits that have been made in a particular period. Winning in options trading is normally reflected by the amounts of profits likely to be received at a particular time.

Below are some of the winning tricks that should be implemented while getting involved in various options trading activities.

The Tips Used in Options Trading

There are several tips that we need to abide by to achieve greatness in several options trading activities, including the following:

Investment tool. Different kinds of options are equated to as ways of risk-reducing kind of investment. By adhering to various options trading strategies that help in managing risks, the trader involved is obliged to invest well in options trading. Every trade measure implemented by the option trader should be measured and considered to be fruitful.

Options Greek. Greeks are a term in the options market that defines the different scales of risks normally involved in options trading. Some of the Greeks involved are a delta, theta, alpha, and so many others that define various risk management portfolios and other options trading activities that need to be exercised. With all these in my mind, your options trading activities are likely to fall out in place and success be greatly pronounced.

Be conversant with the number of contracts involved. Several contracts are normally administered in options trading that contain different kinds of terms and conditions. Get engaged with most of the inexpensive option contracts while selling that are likely to reduce the financial costs of the entire options trading activities.

Capital management. Trading involves the utilization of a specific amount of capital that needs to be used in options trading. Be careful in every move you make with your cash in several options trading activities because acquiring large chunks of losses is and will always be an option in trading. Make sure options trading does not make you broke because of several misuses of funds that can be brought about by bad management of capital.

Exclude expectations. Sometimes it is highly recommended that we do not try and expect any kind of results during options trading. Expected results outcomes to great disappointments. Chances of acquiring loans in options trading are known to be so low though the chances are not zero as you think they are. They are just mere, and with that in mind, you should mind on what you plan to trade with to avoid large loads of losses.

Selling naked options. It is much advisable to sell naked options rather than buying a stock because fewer amounts of risks are likely to be involved hence implying that the amount of monetary value to be lost is estimated to be pretty much less in various options trading activities that are likely to be involved.

Patience. In every trading day, there may be wins and losses. Bad days mean large loads of losses have been made, and a great financial breakdown has been experienced. You should be patient in whatever result you get to experience. Strictly stick to your game plan and follow the various strategies you have outlined. Study every move you make and learn from a great experience. Options trading calls for patience in learning and working things out. Remember that making reckless and inappropriate trading moves should not comfort you that all things are going to be okay with time, be smart.

Risks management. Every option strategy has a well-defined kind of risk. Before you decide on the kind of option you would like to engage in, weigh the risk tolerance of the option and check it corresponds with you. With that in mind, it becomes so much easier to handle and lay some strategies on how to handle your kind of risks.

Dividends. Before initiating an option, check whether the particular option offers dividends to the stock in question during a particular period that is before the expiration date.

Option objective. A set objective thrusts the trader to achieve more and motivates him or her to focus on what he or she wants to benefit from options trading. Set a big goal that should motivate you to work extra hard and achieve large chunks of profits.

Market volatility. This factor is famous for causing large loads of losses where stock prices just keep changing unexpectedly during trading at a particular time. Remember that losses result in a great financial breakdown.

Flexible thinking. The market tends to be as volatile as depicted by the fluctuations of the market prices during trading. Think of the stagnation, rises and falls of the market moves that are likely to occur during a particular options trading period. Thinking flexibly also helps you to be aware of the changes that are likely to occur in the market and the trader gets to implement various strategies.

Calling shots. Options trading gives the trader the chance to purchase and sell stock at their set price within a particular time. The buying, selling, exercising and other activities expose traders to various opportunities in the market during options trading. This should be a great tip and used as one of the ways of making large chunks of profits in options trading.

Know your break-even point. Being conversant with your break-even point by strictly following your laid strategies that should guide you in reaching the specific price and profits be made during a specific trading period.

In-depth research. This talks of conducting wide and extensive research about various options trading strategies and other basic fundamental facts about it. Research allows the trader to get informed about options trading tactics, learn new skills, and improve on the existing skills and master successful trading moves that would result in large amounts of profits.

Escape strategy. Formulating a plan and adhering to it will always bring good news. Always know when to exit the market considering the current status of the market volatility and still stick with the particular set strategies.

Be proactive. This one calls for dynamic nature kind of personality of an options trader where he or she is expected to check up on the trends, research, more learning. Inspect any kind of past losses and note where you messed up and get down into more ways in increasing the chances of losses made. Research, read and always strive for great progress.

Use implied volatility. Implied volatility is the expected volatility of the kind of stock available at the market at a particular time. Implied volatility is influenced by the rates of supply and demand currently happening at the market and as the demand increases during a particular option, the rate of implied volatility rises.

Self-discipline. With self-discipline, a trader is obliged to follow his or her laid strategies all the time despite the market volatility influence. The trader can control the amount of capital involved in trading to avoid major losses that could lead to a great financial breakdown.

How to Learn About Options Trading

Remember that life stops when you stop getting educated. This part will mainly target the novice option traders that are pretty much curious and interested in how they are likely to get involved and get started with options trading. Below are some of the ways that you can consider when learning:

Udemy: Udemy is an online platform rich in educational content in various fields of several life aspects. It contains several videos and writings that may be so educational to the novice and even the experienced options traders. Go through the various learning videos and kindly take down some important notes.

YouTube: YouTube is a common social media platform and pretty much popular. Certain videos containing various levels of options trading are available, that is possible to guide the potential option trader on how to start and look into various ways in which risks are handled in options trading.

Options trading charts: Analyzing options trading charts is also one of the ways that are highly recommended by professional charts. Charts express the general statistics of the actual activities of options trading that is much to the beginners as they try to figure out several strategies that they would like to implement. Charts are also a great help to the experienced traders as they can predict what is likely to happen to the market and decide on where to put their precious money and get good guidance on what they should buy or sell.

Investopedia: This is a common financial website that is also a great learning source for the option traders. It contains various options trading fields with several constructive illustrations that have been presumed to be of great aid. Basic information about options trading to advanced is available and diverse discussions held.

Chart School: This is a general site for charts, where charts are analyzed, with several indicators about the current options trading activities and various chart tools. Charts equip the traders about the actual activities involved in options trading, the current trends and express the volatility of the market.

Articles: Articles have become quite common all over the Internet. Some represent detailed information about various options trading fields, while some traders get to talk of their options trading experiences and so many other things in the world of options trading.

Discussions: Online discussion has been declared as one of the ways of acquiring options trading knowledge and experience as traders get to inquire about various options trading strategies and different ways of handling various risks. Online discussions can be spotted in multiple social media like Quora, Twitter, and more. Experienced traders get to unfold their experience and teach one or two things to the novice.

Conclusion

Real options trading professional uses reasonable cash the board system on each trading chance, weighted against the potential danger of non-execution. This implies a real option dealer will never put all his money into one significant out of the cash position! Practical options trading professional uses exchange investigation strategies dependent on demonstrated procedures to put the chances of execution to support them and never treat each exchange as a 50/50 wager. Real options trading professional compute the measure of options influence to be utilized on each, so his portfolio is never over-utilized. A practical option trading professional don't hope to become wildly successful on his next exchange, and he isn't going for one tremendous grand slam yet a progression of little successes that in the end includes. A real option trading professional never enable one misfortune to clear out his portfolio since he approaches the market with deference realizing that regardless of how much investigation has been led, there is dependably an opportunity that the market will neutralize him.

It will only be a matter of time before you then begin implementing credible strategies for huge rewards. Options trading can be vastly profitable. However, it is sometimes viewed as a double-edged sword because it can sometimes be risky.

The risks only occur when traders do not apply their knowledge or strategies as required. If you come up with a surefire strategy, then you should stick with it to the end. This gives you a much better chance for success so always back-test your strategies and then implement them with confidence.

There are a lot of different market conditions that you could work with when you end up trading in options. Sometimes the market will rise a little or a lot, sometimes they will stay steady, and sometimes they will fall a little or a lot. And with options trading, you are able to make money on all of these conditions if you use the right strategy.

As a beginner, there are a lot of different strategies that are out there that you are able to keep track of and use the way that you want. But all of this information can be a bit confusing when you first get started out. To keep things a bit easier, we are going to take a look at some of the market scenarios that you may run into overtime and how you can pick out the right strategies that will handle these markets and still be successful.

Securities price rises a bit and the first thing that we are going to look at is if the price of your security ends up rising a little bit. There are a few options for strategies that are going to work here including the short put; the bull put spread, and the bull call spread. First is the bull call spread. The advantage of using this strategy is that you are able to reduce some of the costs that you pay upfront but the downside is that there are some limitations on your profits if the asset ends up rising quite a bit.

I hope you have learned something!

Chapter 1. Control Your Emotions

Since trading options is mostly about short time periods, most people have this idea that the prices of options are not going to fluctuate much in that time. But that is wrong, and you need to rethink if you are thinking along those lines as well. If you study past data, you will see that options trading witnesses a lot of fluctuations in price even if it is over a short period of time. So, if you think that options trading mean your money will stay protected, then I have to tell you that you are wrong. Of course, people lose money in options trading, just like investing directly in the stock market. But that does not mean you have to be happy about the fact you are losing money because you will feel low and you will start panicking – that is the NORMAL reaction. But you have to learn how to keep your emotions in check.

You need to learn how to remain calm and observe your emotions from a distance instead of giving in to them. Slowly, you will learn how you can stick it out so that you can see whether or not you get any good returns in the future before the expiration date. Options trading can really be a financial roller coaster. You cannot invest in options with the mentality of a Warren Buffet investor because options do not appreciate in the same manner. A little bit of study would reveal that options increase on a percentage basis, and their movement is way faster than any other type of investment.

For example, if a person has multiple contracts in his/her possession and is trading them all, then they might incur simultaneous losses and profits of $500 each over the course of a few hours. But technically speaking, do not confuse options traders with day traders because they are not, but your mindset should be slightly like that of a day trader if you want to make it big in options trading.

I am going to show you how you can control your emotions even when you are on this rollercoaster ride of options trading.

Getting Started

As a beginner, you will have a tendency to jump into the market right away and begin your journey as a trader. But before you do that, let me remind you of some of the things that are crucial for you to learn. I cannot stress enough on the fact that a good and proper understanding of the basics of options trading is going to get you far in your journey. You also should learn about the different types of options that are present in the market so that you know what you should pick. I know that I have probably told you all of this before, but I am reiterating this for one simple reason, and that is – this is the golden rule about being a top trader. The more you enhance your knowledge about investing, the more will be your chances to get success.

Once you have gone through all the basics and understood them carefully, you will have a clear picture in your head about what you are getting yourself into. The next step is to find your motivation and always hold tightly to it because, in trading, beginners tend to lose that motivation very fast. You need to ask yourself exactly how much money do you think about making. The figure will vary from person to person, and although there is no limit to this, you should still be realistic about it. No one becomes a billionaire overnight. You should also ask yourself how you plan to spend or use that money once you have earned it. This is where you are going to find your motivation because you are setting goals or you have some dreams that you want to fulfill, and so you will try your best to make those dreams come true. When you are in the thick of the trading, this motivation is going to keep you going and also help you stay focused on the trade.

When you have the trading plan ready, it will constantly tell you about the things that you should achieve in a trade. Some of the common things that are included in a trading plan are – your goals, your idea of what is going to happen, the strategies that you want to use, and any other note or guideline that you think might be of use to you. All of this together is going to make you successful. You will be putting yourself into a risky endeavor if you start trading without having this plan ready.

Never Make Emotional Decisions

As you must have understood by now that options are very volatile in nature, and depending on certain stocks, it can get really very volatile. There are so many beginner traders who come into options trading but then become emotional because it is not what they thought it would be. And this is exactly what I am talking about. This approach will not do any good to you, and that is why prior research is necessary to know the waters you are stepping into.

In most cases, people exit at the wrong time just because they became emotional and overwhelmed during the trade, but only if they had stayed a bit longer or if they had made their exit a bit early, they would have been able to make a lump sum profit. If you are trading options, your worst mistake would be to make any sudden moves. That is why a trading plan is so necessary so that you can have all the rules at hand on when do you need to exit or enter a trade. And all you have to do is stick to those rules.

The tides in the financial market keep changing, and if you want to navigate them like a pro, then active monitoring is important. There will come a time when you will feel like giving in to your behavioral impulses, but you have to stop yourself right there and take a step back to analyze the situation in front of you. The market ups and downs can easily make you start practicing emotional buying and selling if you are not careful. And the usual trend shows that whenever the market is good, investors have the tendency of piling into investments and then they sell at the bottom. This is mostly because of the fear and hype generated by media.

There are several theories that have been proposed about investor behavior because it is something that is being studied extensively. But if we look at the real-life situation, you will understand that trading can bring about stress, and in situations of extreme stress, it is quite common for rational thinking to be clouded by the investor's psyche. The stress can not only be a result of panic but also euphoria. That is why I have told you time and again that the approach towards investing should be realistic and rational. Never underestimate risk management because every investment has its own risks, and if you do not gauge those risks, then you are the one who will be at a loss.

There are so many non-professional investors in the market who actually use their hard-earned money for trading just because they think they are going to receive a huge return. But sometimes market developments can lead them to lose their money, and it is very painful indeed. All of this leads to extreme stress and that stress, in turn, can lead to second-guessing every step. That is why you need to identify what your risk tolerance is so that you do not end up making emotional decisions when these risks become unbearable for you.

Be a Bit Math-Oriented

If you are not good with numbers or if you are shy about it, then you are not going to do well in options trading. This is because it is entirely a game of numbers. But don't get me wrong, I am not asking you to go to some renowned university to get a degree in mathematics or statistics. You can read a bit by yourself and get a grasp on the basic concepts because a little bit of knowledge about statistics and probability will do you good in the long term and make you better than the others in the world of options trading. To be honest, I don't know how you are going to get to the top if you do not know the basics of statistics. The core of options trading will always have some Maths in it, and you cannot go around it in any way.

Also, when you are math-oriented, you will have a better understanding of the market, and you will see options in a different light. You will learn to analyze the situations and markets before going all-in with your capital. This, in turn, will also make strategizing an easier process.

Maintain Trading Journals

When you have a trading journal, keeping track of your trade becomes way easier. Your brokerage statement is not going to include everything, whereas your trading journal will have all those details, making it easier for you. It will also remind you of the mistakes you made in a certain market condition. Do you know how this is going to benefit you? If that same market condition were to repeat itself, you know exactly what strategy you will not be using, and this will help you not to make the same mistake again. You can also keep track of every time you became emotional and what triggered you. This is will not prevent you from becoming emotional but it will remind you of the loss you incurred and this probably will help you get a grip on yourself.

When you record your trades and make notes in your journal, you get a clear picture of the situation you are in. Yes, sometimes, that picture can be wrong, and this does not mean that you have to back out. A losing record is simply when you have to find out where you are going wrong and why you are not making profits from the trade. All of this will become easier because you have written your steps in the trading journal. And then all you have to make is adjustments.

Lightning Source UK Ltd.
Milton Keynes UK
UKHW020648230321
380841UK00011B/228